Simone Biles

Jackie Golusky

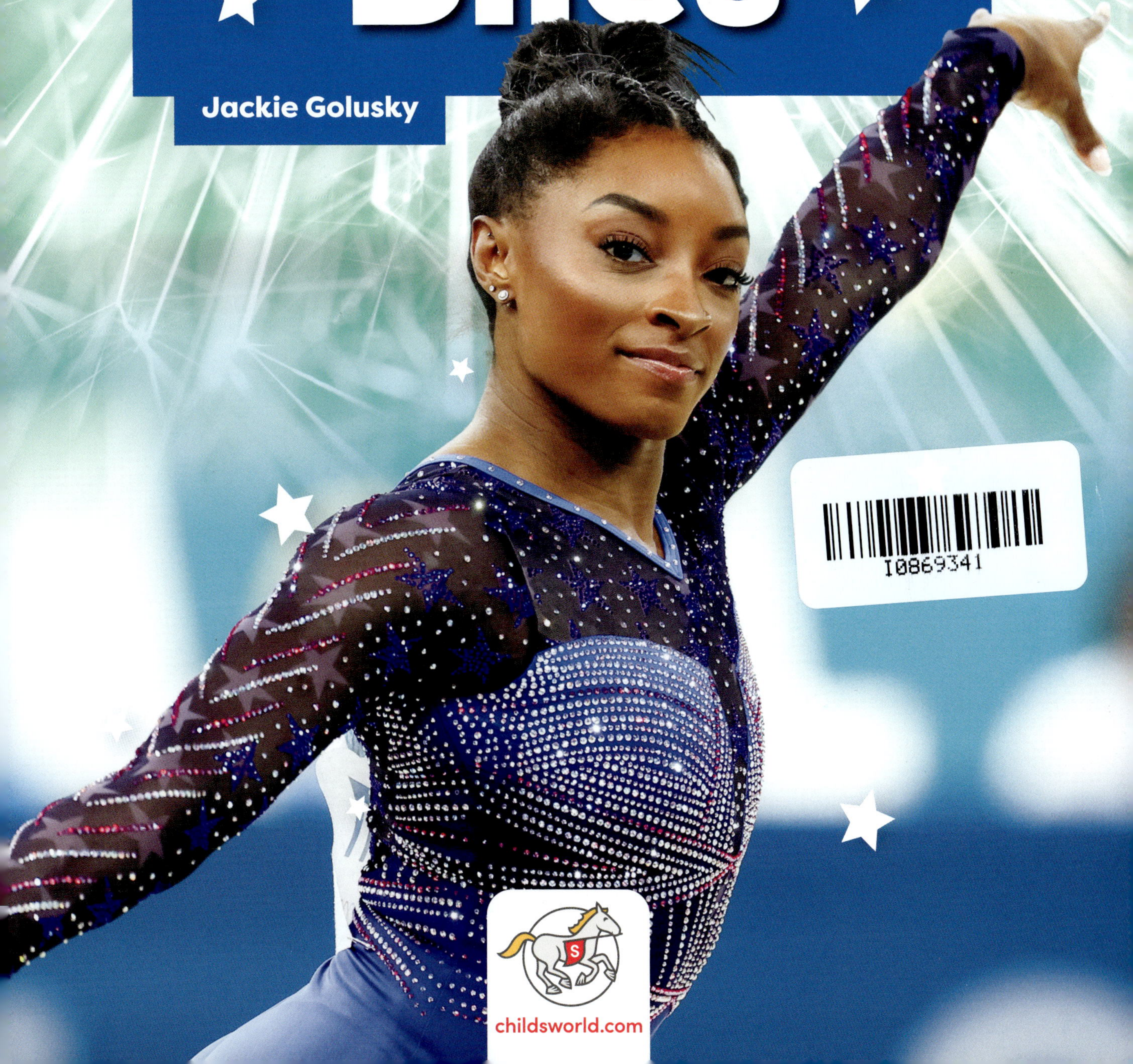

childsworld.com

The Child's World
childsworld.com

Published by The Child's World®
800-599-READ • www.childsworld.com

Photography Credits
Photographs ©: Pete Dovgan/Speed Media/Icon Sportswire/AP Images, cover, 1; Ezra Shaw/Getty Images Sport/Getty Images, 5; Shutterstock Images, 7, 13, 15, 19, 26, 29; Naomi Baker/Getty Images Sport/Getty Images, 8; Chris Pizzello/AP Images, 11; Gerlach Delissen/Corbis Sport/Getty Images, 16; Richard Blumenthal/Wikimedia Commons, 21; Alex Wong/Getty Images News/Getty Images, 22; Michael Reaves/Getty Images Sport/Getty Images, 25; Design elements from Shutterstock Images

ISBN Information
9781503875722 (Reinforced Library Binding)
9781503876705 (Portable Document Format)
9781503877207 (Online Multi-user eBook)
9781503877825 (Electronic Publication)

LCCN 2025938202

Printed in the United States of America

BRINGING THE WORLD TO YOUNG READERS 1968

ABOUT THE AUTHOR

Jackie Golusky is a writer who lives near the Twin Cities in Minnesota. She graduated from Hamline University with a degree in creative writing. Her cat, Remmy, is her writing companion.

TABLE of CONTENTS

CHAPTER ONE

The G.O.A.T.

Simone Biles waited her turn at the vault. The American gymnast was competing in the team event at the Tokyo Olympic Games in 2021. Biles ran toward the vault and pushed off. But something went wrong. Biles was supposed to complete two and a half twists in the air. But she got through only one and a half. She barely landed. Biles was feeling what gymnasts call "the twisties." This sensation makes it dangerous to compete. Gymnasts lose track of where they are in the air.

Landing inside the lines after springing off the vault table earns athletes higher scores.

Biles made a shocking decision. She pulled out of the team event. She did not feel safe competing. She spoke out on the importance of **mental health**. Doctors, gymnasts, and many others applauded Biles for focusing on her well-being.

IN HER WORDS

In an interview at the Tokyo Olympic Games in 2021, Biles talked about her decision to pull out of the competition:

> **"I say put mental health first. Because if you don't, then you're not going to enjoy your sport and you're not going to succeed as much as you want to. So it's okay sometimes to even sit out the big competitions to focus on yourself, because it shows how strong of a competitor and person that you really are—rather than just battle through it."**

Source: Chappell, Bill. "Read What Simone Biles Said After Her Withdrawal from the Olympic Final." NPR, *July 28, 2021. www.npr.org.*

In June 2024, the US Gymnastics Championship took place in Fort Worth, Texas, at the Dickies Arena.

Three years later, all eyes were on Biles at the Paris Olympic Games. Some fans wondered how Biles would perform. Gymnastics is a very demanding sport, and Biles could feel the toll on her body. But earlier in 2024, Biles had claimed a historic ninth **all-around** title at the US Gymnastics Championship.

In Paris, Biles started the team all-around event strong. She performed a move she created, known as the Biles II. It was the world's most difficult vault. Her impressive vault performance gave the US team the lead.

Jordan Chiles, Suni Lee, Simone Biles, Hezly Rivera, and Jade Carey (from left to right) made up the 2024 US women's gymnastics team.

Biles and her teammates competed in various events. As the competition neared the end, it was up to Biles to secure the win. She took to the balance beam. Biles stunned as she completed a triple-twisting double backflip. She needed about nine points to win. Her score was almost 15 points! She claimed the gold for her team and nation.

Biles's winning streak was not over yet. She quickly led the competition in the individual all-around. She had a narrow lead going into her strongest event, the floor exercise. After jumping and flipping on the floor, Biles smiled. She left the mat holding up her finger to indicate number one. She claimed the gold by just over one point. After her win, Biles put on a diamond goat necklace. It was a nod to people calling her the Greatest of All Time (G.O.A.T.).

With 11 Olympic medals and 30 World Championship medals, Biles is the most decorated gymnast in history. Biles's determination and skill have brought her to the world's biggest stages. She invented moves that no one else has been able to land. Biles has completely reshaped the sport of gymnastics.

SCORING IN GYMNASTICS

Gymnastics judges consider the execution and difficulty of a routine. Execution means how well moves were done. That score starts at 10.0 points. Gymnasts lose points for making mistakes. The difficulty score starts at 0. Gymnasts earn points based on how difficult their routine is. For team scores, the top three scores per event are added together.

CHAPTER TWO

Start of an Iconic Career

On March 14, 1997, Simone Arianne Biles was born in Columbus, Ohio. Simone's **birth parents** are Shannon Biles and Kelvin Clemons. Simone had two older siblings, Ashley and Tevin. When Simone was 2 years old, her younger sister Adria was born.

Shannon and Kelvin struggled with addiction. Addiction is a **disease** that makes people feel a need for something harmful, such as alcohol or drugs. Similar to other illnesses, treatment can help people get better.

When Simone was 3, she and her siblings entered foster care. Children are placed in foster care when their caregivers cannot take care of them. Sometimes children return to their caregivers. Other times they may be adopted by a family member or another adult.

Biles's family members have been some of her biggest supporters. Ronald, Nellie, and Adria (far right) attended an event for the release of Biles's Netflix documentary.

Simone's grandparents adopted her and Adria when Simone was 6. Ronald and Nellie Biles lived in Spring, Texas. Simone and Adria moved to be with them. Ashley and Tevin wanted to stay in Ohio, so they were adopted by their aunt.

Simone had another life-changing event when she was 6. She went on a field trip to Bannon's Gymnastix. Simone had never done gymnastics before. But she loved jumping and running. She copied the teenagers who were training. Coach Aimee Boorman saw Simone's talent. The gym sent a letter home with Simone. They encouraged her family to sign her up for gymnastics classes.

Simone started training at Bannon's. Boorman coached the young gymnast. Simone succeeded in executing moves. But she had a hard time focusing. She was diagnosed with attention deficit hyperactivity disorder (ADHD). ADHD is a disorder that affects a person's ability to pay attention or focus. Simone started taking medication. This helped her focus better at school and in the gym.

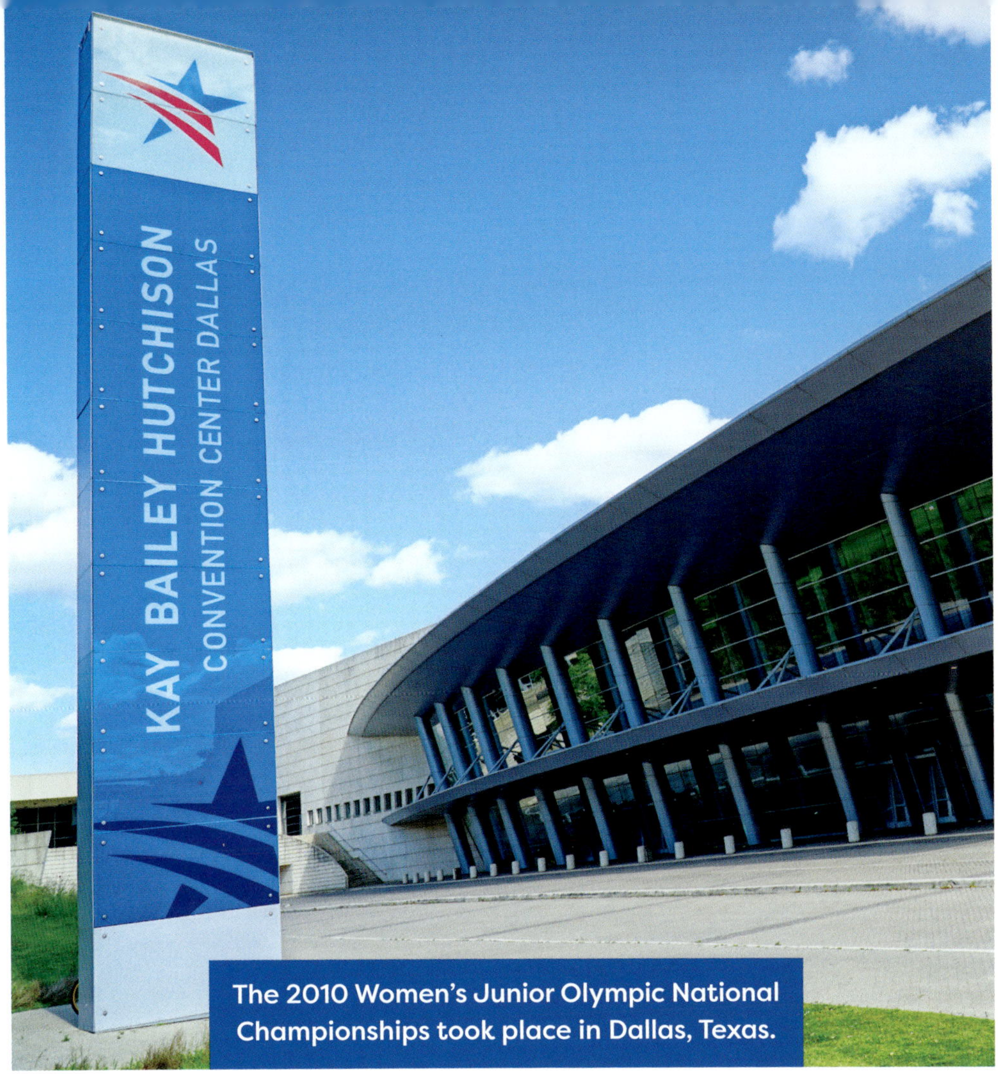

The 2010 Women's Junior Olympic National Championships took place in Dallas, Texas.

By middle school, Simone was training up to 20 hours per week. At 13 years old, Simone competed in the 2010 Women's Junior Olympic National Championships. Many gymnasts who perform well in the competition continue their careers into college. Some reach the Olympic Games. Simone did not hold back. Her vault earned her a bronze medal. She won gold for the floor exercise.

In 2011, Simone competed at the American Classic. Judges were impressed by the difficulty of Simone's moves. She claimed gold in vault and bronze in the all-around. Simone's performance **qualified** her for a competition that determined which gymnasts would join the US National Team. She finished in 14th place and did not make the team.

At 14 years old, Simone had a decision to make. If she wanted to do gymnastics full-time, she would have to be homeschooled. Simone worried about missing out on high school with her friends. But she decided to focus on gymnastics. Ronald became Simone's teacher. He taught Simone between workouts.

In 2012, Simone dazzled at the US Classic. She landed the Yurchenko 2.5, also called the Amanar, on vault. Simone took home the junior all-around title. She was too young to qualify for the Olympics that year. But Simone's career was just starting.

In Yurchenko vaults, gymnasts use a back handspring to push off the vaulting table. Because the gymnast is facing backward when pushing off, this style of vault can be difficult to master.

Simone performs her floor routine during the Artistic Gymnastics World Championship in 2013.

CHAPTER THREE

A World Champion

Simone had a difficult start to 2013. At the US Classic, she fell during her floor routine. She also had difficulty on the balance beam. Simone's coach removed her from competition. The young gymnast saw a **sports psychologist**. Simone learned to not care about others' expectations and to focus on her performance.

Three weeks after the US Classic, Simone competed in the USA Gymnastics National Championship. She won silver medals for balance beam, vault, uneven bars, and floor exercise. Simone also won the individual all-around, beating 2012 Olympic gold medalist Kyla Ross.

Simone's thrilling performance earned her a spot on the US National Team. Two months later, she headed to Belgium for the World Championships. Simone was competing against the best gymnasts in the world. But she stunned judges with her high jumps, quick turns, and secure landings. Simone became the first Black American woman to claim the all-around title.

The next year, Simone defended her title. The gymnast also led Team USA to gold in the team all-around. Simone returned to the World Championships in 2015. She claimed another individual all-around title. This made her the first woman in history to claim three world all-around titles in a row. She also had 14 medals from the World Championships. This was the highest number held by a US gymnast. Ten of her medals were gold, the most claimed by a female gymnast. Many people were wondering how many medals Simone would win at her first Olympic Games.

Biles performs on the balance beam at the 2016 Olympics.

Simone's first event at the 2016 Olympics was the team all-around. She completed a Yurchenko 2.5 on vault. In the floor exercise, she landed a half-twist without being able to see the ground. She was the first gymnast to ever land the move in an **elite** competition. Her amazing performance helped lead Team USA to gold.

But Simone was just getting started. She earned top scores for vault, floor exercise, and balance beam to win gold in the individual all-around. She also claimed gold in vault and floor exercise. Simone won bronze on the balance beam.

Simone was thrilled about her wins. But, after the Olympics, she realized she had achieved her goals at 19 years old. She was not sure what to do with the rest of her life. She struggled with **depression**. In 2017, Simone took time off from training.

In that same year, news shocked the gymnastics world. Simone's teammate Aly Raisman spoke out about being abused by a team doctor. The doctor had been inappropriately touching female gymnasts for years. After hearing other gymnasts tell their stories, Simone decided to share her own. More than 150 gymnasts said that they had been abused by that doctor. The doctor was sentenced to life in prison.

OPENING A NEW GYM

Over the years, Simone switched gyms to keep training with Boorman. In 2014, Ronald and Nellie Biles opened their own gym, World Champions Centre (WCC). Nellie had the idea to build a gym for Simone and other gymnasts. Boorman came and worked at WCC, where Simone trained. The gym holds classes to build gymnastics skills. It hosts summer day camps for young athletes.

Biles and other female gymnasts shared their stories of abuse with the US Senate. Senator Richard Blumenthal (center) also spoke at the hearing.

After almost 2 years, Simone returned to competing. She wore a teal leotard at the USA Gymnastics National Championship. Teal is the color for supporting sexual assault survivors. Simone won four gold medals.

During the 2018 World Championships, Biles had a kidney stone. This is a hard object that forms in the kidneys. Kidney stones can be extremely painful. But Simone fought through the pain. She won the individual all-around, vault, and floor exercise. She also got silver for the uneven bars and bronze for balance beam.

Biles met President Barack Obama and First Lady Michelle Obama in 2016.

The following year at the World Championships, Simone completed a double-twisting double backflip off the balance beam. During floor exercise, she performed a triple-twisting double backflip. It was the first time she had done the moves in a competition. Both moves would be named after her. Simone won five gold medals. She now had a total of 25 medals from the World Championships. Simone was the competition's most decorated gymnast. She had come far. But Simone already had her sights on the next Olympic Games.

CHAPTER FOUR

Flipping the Script

The Tokyo Olympic Games were scheduled for 2020. But the COVID-19 **pandemic** delayed the games until 2021. Schools and businesses closed to prevent the spread of the illness. This meant Biles had time off from training. She spent a lot of time with her boyfriend, Jonathan Owens. Biles met the professional football player in March of 2020.

Biles started to train in the spring of 2021. She had plans to compete in the US Classic in June 2021. It was the first time Owens saw her compete. Ronald and Nellie were also cheering her on. They had never missed one of Biles's competitions. Biles won the all-around and became the first woman to win seven all-around titles at the competition.

In February 2022, Jonathan Owens proposed to Biles. They got married later that year.

The following month, Biles traveled to Tokyo for the Olympic Games. Because of COVID-19, none of Biles's loved ones could cheer for her in person. When she struggled at the competition, she could not see her supporters. Biles had to pull out of the team all-around competition. The US team still won silver. Some people criticized Biles for pulling out of the Olympics. They thought she let her team down. But many more were supportive. Biles was able to compete in the individual balance beam event. She won bronze. Biles said the bronze medal meant more to her than all her gold medals.

Biles pulled out of other events at the Tokyo Olympics, but she still competed on the balance beam. This event did not have the twisting elements that gave her trouble elsewhere.

After a break from gymnastics, Biles returned to the World Championships in 2023. She won silver on vault. And she claimed gold in the team and individual all-arounds, floor exercise, and balance beam. She now had a record-breaking 30 medals, with 23 of them being gold.

Biles was headed back to the Olympic Games. The 2024 competition was in Paris, France. Biles called the competition her "**redemption** tour." She wanted to prove she still could compete at a high level. With Owens, Ronald, and Nellie watching, Biles stunned as she claimed gold in the all-around.

MOVES NAMED AFTER BILES

Simone Biles has created five gymnastic moves. These are named after her. They are the Biles I (floor), the Biles II (floor), the Biles I (vault), the Biles II (vault), and the Biles (beam). The Biles II floor exercise features two flips and three twists. On balance beam, the Biles is a double-twisting double backflip.

Two days later, she completed the Biles II on vault and won another gold medal. On August 5, the gymnast claimed a silver medal for her floor exercise. While Biles did not win, she still made history. It was the first time the Olympics had an all-Black **podium** in gymnastics history. Brazil's Rebeca Andrade took gold and US teammate Jordan Chiles took bronze. Biles and Chiles bowed to Andrade, who held her hands up in celebration.

Biles's success in Paris made her the most decorated US Olympic gymnast. People wondered if she might earn even more. The next Olympics would be held in Los Angeles, California, in 2028. In a 2025 interview, Biles said she hoped she would be there. Whether she would be competing or behind the scenes, fans looked forward to seeing what Biles would do next. The gymnast had redefined the sport. It was easy to see why Biles is called the G.O.A.T.

BILES'S OLYMPIC MEDALS

Simone Biles has earned many medals in her Olympic gymnastics career.

4 medals at Rio 2016
- Floor exercise
- Individual all-around
- Team all-around
- Vault

3 medals at Paris 2024
- Individual all-around
- Team all-around
- Vault

1 medal at Tokyo 2020 (2021)
- Team all-around

1 medal at Paris 2024
- Floor exercise

1 medal at Rio 2016
- Balance beam

1 medal at Tokyo 2020 (2021)
- Balance beam

GLOSSARY

all-around (ALL-uh-rownd) All-around is a combined score in women's gymnastics for vault, uneven bars, balance beam, and floor exercise. Biles has won gold for the team all-around and individual all-around.

birth parents (BERTH PAYR-unts) Birth parents are the natural parents of a child. Biles's birth parents are Shannon Biles and Kelvin Clemons.

depression (dih-PREH-shun) Depression is a medical condition that often results in sadness, a lack of interest in activities, tiredness, and trouble focusing. Biles struggled with depression after the 2016 Olympics.

disease (dih-ZEEZ) A disease is a condition that stops the body's regular functions. Addiction is a type of disease.

elite (uh-LEET) Someone or something elite is of the highest quality. Biles competed in many elite competitions.

mental health (MEN-tuhl HELTH) Mental health is how well someone is doing mentally and emotionally. Biles brought attention to athletes' mental health.

pandemic (pan-DEH-muk) A pandemic is an outbreak of a disease that spreads across many places. The COVID-19 pandemic shut down schools and businesses.

podium (POH-dee-uhm) In sports, a podium is a raised platform where athletes receive awards. At the Paris 2024 Olympics, it was the first time there was an all-Black podium in gymnastics history.

qualified (KWAA-luh-fide) People who qualified have met different standards of performance. In 2011, Biles qualified for a competition to determine which gymnasts would join the US national team.

redemption (ruh-DEMP-shun) Redemption is a process of coming back, usually stronger. Biles called the 2024 Olympics her redemption tour.

sports psychologist (SPORTZ sy-KAH-luh-jist) A sports psychologist is a person who helps athletes with any mental health concerns they have. Biles met with a sports psychologist.

FAST FACTS

- ★ On March 14, 1997, Simone Arianne Biles was born. Simone and her three siblings were placed in foster care when she was 3 years old. Simone and her younger sister, Adria, were later adopted by their grandparents.
- ★ Simone first tried gymnastics on a field trip to a gym. Coaches noticed her talent and encouraged her parents to sign her up for gymnastics. Simone started gymnastics at 6 years old.
- ★ Biles is known as the G.O.A.T., or Greatest of All Time. She won 11 medals over three Olympic Games. Biles also holds 30 World Championships medals, 23 of which are gold.
- ★ Biles has created five gymnastics moves that are named after her. She has two moves on floor exercise, two on vault, and one on the balance beam.
- ★ Biles brought attention to athletes' mental health during the Tokyo Olympic Games. She pulled out of the competition when a condition made it too dangerous for her to compete.

ONE STRIDE FURTHER

- ★ Biles was noticed for her gymnastics abilities. Do you have special talents or skills? How do you strengthen these skills?
- ★ During the Tokyo Olympic Games, Biles realized that it would not be safe for her to compete. She pulled out of the event. Have you ever had a moment when you realized something was not working for you? What did you do?
- ★ Biles has felt pressure to succeed throughout her life. Have you ever felt pressured? How do you deal with this pressure?

FIND OUT MORE

IN THE LIBRARY

Lawrence, Blythe. *Trailblazing Women in Gymnastics.* Chicago, IL: Norwood House Press, 2023.

Loh, Stefanie. *Who Is Simone Biles?* New York, NY: Penguin Random House, 2023.

Magoon, Kekla. *She Persisted: Simone Biles.* New York, NY: Philomel, 2023.

ON THE WEB

Visit our website for links about Simone Biles:

childsworld.com/links

Note to Parents, Caregivers, Teachers, and Librarians: We routinely verify our web links to make sure they are safe and active sites. So encourage your readers to check them out!

INDEX